Favorite Christmas Poems

Edited by
James Daley

DOVER PUBLICATIONS, INC.
Mineola, New York

Copyright

Copyright © 2006 by Dover Publications, Inc.
All rights reserved.

Bibliographical Note

This Dover edition, first published in 2006, is a new compilation of fifty-two poems, mostly British and American (plus one German and one Canadian), from the sixteenth to the twentieth centuries.

Library of Congress Cataloging-in-Publication Data

Favorite Christmas poems / edited by James Daley.
     p. cm.
   ISBN 0-486-44746-4 (pbk.)
    1. Christmas—Poetry. 2. Christian poetry, English. 3. Christian poetry, American. I. Daley, James.

PR1195.C49F38 2006
821.008'0334—dc22

2005056038

Manufactured in the United States of America
Dover Publications, Inc., 31 East 2nd Street, Mineola, N.Y. 11501

Contents

Favorite Christmas Poems

Gabriel's Message

SABINE BARING-GOULD (1834–1924)

The angel Gabriel from heaven came,
His wings as drifted snow, his eyes as flame;
"All hail," said he, "thou lowly maiden Mary,
Most highly favoured lady,
    Gloria!

"For know a blessèd mother thou shalt be,
All generations laud and honour thee,
Thy son shall be Emmanuel, by seers foretold.
Most highly favoured lady,
    Gloria!"

Then gentle Mary meekly bowed her head,
"To me be as it pleaseth God," she said,
"My soul shall laud and magnify his holy name."
Most highly favoured lady,
    Gloria!

Of her, Emmanuel, the Christ, was born
In Bethlehem, all on a Christmas morn,
And Christian folk throughout the world will ever say,
"Most highly favoured lady,
    Gloria!"

Noel: Christmas Eve, 1913
Pax hominibus benae voluntatis

ROBERT BRIDGES (1844–1930)

A frosty Christmas Eve
   when the stars were shining
Fared I forth alone
   where westward falls the hill,
And from many a village
   in the water'd valley
Distant music reach'd me
   peals of bells aringing:
The constellated sounds
   ran sprinkling on earth's floor
As the dark vault above
   with stars was spangled o'er.

Then sped my thought to keep
   that first Christmas of all
When the shepherds watching
   by their folds ere the dawn
Heard music in the fields
   and marveling could not tell
Whether it were angels
   or the bright stars singing.

Now blessed be the tow'rs
   that crown England so fair
That stand up strong in prayer
   unto God for our souls:
Blessed be their founders
   (said I) an' our country folk
Who are ringing for Christ
   in the belfries to-night
With arms lifted to clutch
   the rattling ropes that race

Into the dark above
   and the mad romping din.

But to me heard afar
   it was starry music
Angels' song, comforting
   as the comfort of Christ
When he spake tenderly
   to his sorrowful flock:
The old words came to me
   by the riches of time
Mellow'd and transfigured
   as I stood on the hill
Heark'ning in the aspect
   of th' eternal silence.

O Little Town of Bethlehem
BISHOP PHILLIPS BROOKS (1835–1893)

O little town of Bethlehem,
   How still we see thee lie!
Above thy deep and dreamless sleep
   The silent stars go by.
Yet in thy dark streets shineth
   The everlasting light;
The hopes and fears of all the years
   Are met in thee to-night.

O morning stars, together
   Proclaim the holy birth,
And praises sing to God the King,
   And peace to men on earth;
For Christ is born of Mary;
   And, gathered all above,
While mortals sleep, the angels keep
   Their watch of wondering love.

How silently, how silently,
   The wondrous gift is given!
So God imparts to human hearts
   The blessings of his heaven.
No ear may hear his coming;
   But in this world of sin,
Where meek souls will receive him, still
   The dear Christ enters in.

Where children pure and happy
   Pray to the blessèd Child,
Where misery cries out to thee,
   Son of the mother mild;
Where charity stands watching
   And faith holds wide the door,
The dark night wakes, the glory breaks,
   And Christmas comes once more.

O holy Child of Bethlehem,
  Descend to us, we pray;
Cast out our sin, and enter in,
  Be born in us to-day.
We hear the Christmas Angels
  The great glad tidings tell:
O come to us, abide with us,
  Our Lord Emmanuel.

Christmas Song

BLISS CARMAN (1861–1929)

Above the weary waiting world,
Asleep in chill despair,
There breaks a sound of joyous bells
Upon the frosted air.
And o'er the humblest rooftree, lo,
A star is dancing on the snow.

What makes the yellow star to dance
Upon the brink of night?
What makes the breaking dawn to glow
So magically bright,—
And all the earth to be renewed
With infinite beatitude?

The singing bells, the throbbing star,
The sunbeams on the snow,
And the awakening heart that leaps
New ecstasy to know,—
They all are dancing in the morn
Because a little child is born.

Christmas Greeting from a Fairy to a Child

LEWIS CARROLL (1832–1898)

Lady, dear, if Fairies may
   For a moment lay aside
Cunning tricks and elfish play,
   'Tis at happy Christmas-tide.

We have heard the children say—
   Gentle children, whom we love—
Long ago on Christmas Day,
   Came a message from above.

Still, as Christmas-tide comes round,
   They remember it again—
Echo still the joyful sound
   "Peace on earth, good-will to men!"

Yet the hearts must childlike be
   Where such heavenly guests abide;
Unto children, in their glee,
   All the year is Christmas-tide!

Thus, forgetting tricks and play
   For a moment, Lady dear,
We would wish you, if we may,
   Merry Christmas, glad New Year!

A Christmas Carol

G. K. CHESTERTON (1874–1936)

The Christ-child lay on Mary's lap,
  His hair was like a light.
(O weary, weary were the world,
  But here is all aright.)

The Christ-child lay on Mary's breast,
  His hair was like a star.
(O stern and cunning are the kings,
  But here the true hearts are.)

The Christ-child lay on Mary's heart,
  His hair was like a fire.
(O weary, weary is the world,
  But here the world's desire.)

The Christ-child stood at Mary's knee,
  His hair was like a crown,
And all the flowers looked up at him,
  And all the stars looked down.

The House of Christmas
G. K. CHESTERTON (1874–1936)

There fared a mother driven forth
Out of an inn to roam;
In the place where she was homeless
All men are at home.
The crazy stable close at hand,
With shaking timber and shifting sand,
Grew a stronger thing to abide and stand
Than the square stones of Rome.

For men are homesick in their homes,
And strangers under the sun,
And they lay their heads in a foreign land
Whenever the day is done.
Here we have battle and blazing eyes,
And chance and honour and high surprise,
But our homes are under miraculous skies
Where the yule tale was begun.

A Child in a foul stable,
Where the beasts feed and foam;
Only where He was homeless
Are you and I at home;
We have hands that fashion and heads that know,
But our hearts we lost—how long ago!
In a place no chart nor ship can show
Under the sky's dome.

This world is wild as an old wives' tale,
And strange the plain things are,
The earth is enough and the air is enough
For our wonder and our war;
But our rest is as far as the fire-drake swings
And our peace is put in impossible things
Where clashed and thundered unthinkable wings
Round an incredible star.

To an open house in the evening
Home shall men come,
To an older place than Eden
And a taller town than Rome.
To the end of the way of the wandering star,
To the things that cannot be and that are,
To the place where God was homeless
And all men are at home.

December

JOHN CLARE (1793–1864)

Glad Christmas comes, and every hearth
   Makes room to give him welcome now,
E'en want will dry its tears in mirth,
   And crown him with a holly bough;
Though tramping 'neath a winter sky,
   O'er snowy paths and rimy stiles,
The housewife sets her spinning by
   To bid him welcome with her smiles.

Each house is swept the day before,
   And windows stuck with ever-greens,
The snow is besom'd from the door,
   And comfort crowns the cottage scenes.
Gilt holly, with its thorny pricks,
   And yew and box, with berries small,
These deck the unused candlesticks,
   And pictures hanging by the wall.

Neighbours resume their annual cheer,
   Wishing, with smiles and spirits high,
Glad Christmas and a happy year,
   To every morning passer-by;
Milkmaids their Christmas journeys go,
   Accompanied with favour'd swain;
And children pace the crumping snow,
   To taste their granny's cake again.

The shepherd, now no more afraid,
   Since custom doth the chance bestow,
Starts up to kiss the giggling maid
   Beneath the branch of mistletoe
That 'neath each cottage beam is seen,
   With pearl-like berries shining gay;
The shadow still of what hath been,
   Which fashion yearly fades away.

The singing wates, a merry throng,
    At early morn, with simple skill,
Yet imitate the angels song,
    And chant their Christmas ditty still;
And, 'mid the storm that dies and swells
    By fits—in hummings softly steals
The music of the village bells,
    Ringing round their merry peals.

When this is past, a merry crew,
    Bedeck'd in masks and ribbons gay,
The "Morris-dance," their sports renew,
    And act their winter evening play.
The clown turn'd king, for penny-praise,
    Storms with the actor's strut and swell;
And Harlequin, a laugh to raise,
    Wears his hunch-back and tinkling bell.

And oft for pence and spicy ale,
    With winter nosegays pinn'd before,
The wassail-singer tells her tale,
    And drawls her Christmas carols o'er.
While 'prentice boy, with ruddy face,
    And rime-bepowder'd, dancing locks,
From door to door with happy pace,
    Runs round to claim his "Christmas box."

The block upon the fire is put,
    To sanction custom's old desires;
And many a fagot's bands are cut,
    For the old farmers' Christmas fires;
Where loud-tongued Gladness joins the throng,
    And Winter meets the warmth of May,
Till feeling soon the heat too strong,
    He rubs his shins, and draws away.

While snows the window-panes bedim,
    The fire curls up a sunny charm,
Where, creaming o'er the pitcher's rim,
    The flowering ale is set to warm;

Mirth, full of joy as summer bees,
    Sits there, its pleasures to impart,
And children, 'tween their parent's knees,
    Sing scraps of carols o'er by heart.

And some, to view the winter weathers,
    Climb up the window-seat with glee,
Likening the snow to falling feathers,
    In Fancy's infant ecstasy;
Laughing, with superstitious love,
    O'er visions wild that youth supplies,
Of people pulling geese above,
    And keeping Christmas in the skies.

As tho' the homestead trees were drest,
    In lieu of snow, with dancing leaves;
As tho' the sun-dried martin's nest,
    Instead of i'cles hung the eaves;
The children hail the happy day—
    As if the snow were April's grass,
And pleas'd, as 'neath the warmth of May,
    Sport o'er the water froze to glass.

Thou day of happy sound and mirth,
    That long with childish memory stays,
How blest around the cottage hearth
    I met thee in my younger days!
Harping, with rapture's dreaming joys,
    On presents which thy coming found,
The welcome sight of little toys,
    The Christmas gift of cousins round.

The wooden horse with arching head,
    Drawn upon wheels around the room;
The gilded coach of gingerbread,
    And many-colour'd sugar plum;
Gilt cover'd books for pictures sought,
    Or stories childhood loves to tell,
With many an urgent promise bought,
    To get to-morrow's lesson well.

And many a thing, a minute's sport,
  Left broken on the sanded floor,
When we would leave our play, and court
  Our parents' promises for more.
Tho' manhood bids such raptures die,
  And throws such toys aside as vain,
Yet memory loves to turn her eye,
  And count past pleasures o'er again.

Around the glowing hearth at night,
  The harmless laugh and winter tale
Go round, while parting friends delight
  To toast each other o'er their ale;
The cotter oft with quiet zeal
  Will musing o'er his Bible lean;
While in the dark the lovers steal
  To kiss and toy behind the screen.

Old customs! Oh! I love the sound,
  However simple they may be:
Whate'er with time hath sanction found,
  Is welcome, and is dear to me.
Pride grows above simplicity,
  And spurns them from her haughty mind,
And soon the poet's song will be
  The only refuge they can find.

A Christmas Carol

SAMUEL TAYLOR COLERIDGE (1772–1834)

The shepherds went their hasty way,
    And found the lowly stable-shed
Where the virgin-mother lay:
    And now they checked their eager tread,
For to the babe, that at her bosom clung,
A mother's song the virgin-mother sung.

They told her how a glorious light,
    Streaming from a heavenly throng,
Around them shone, suspending night;
    While sweeter than a mother's song,
Blessed angels heralded the Saviour's birth,
Glory to God on high! and peace on earth.

She listened to the tale divine,
    And closer still the babe she pressed;
And while she cried, "The babe is mine!"
    The milk rushed faster to her breast:
Joy rose within her, like a summer's morn:
Peace, peace on earth! the Prince of peace is born.

Thou mother of the Prince of peace,
    Poor, simple, and of low estate;
That strife should vanish, battle cease,
    Oh! why should this thy soul elate?
Sweet music's loudest note, the poet's story,
Didst thou ne'er love to hear of fame and glory?

And is not War a youthful king,
    A stately hero clad in mail?
Beneath his footsteps laurels spring;
    Him earth's majestic monarchs hail!
Their friend, their playmate! and his bold bright eye
Compels the maiden's love-confessing sigh.

"Tell this in some more courtly scene,
    To maids and youths in robes of state!
I am a woman poor and mean,
    And therefore is my soul elate.
War is a ruffian, all with guilt defiled,
That from the aged father tears his child!

"A murderous fiend, by fiends adored,
    He kills the sire and starves the son,
The husband kills, and from her board
    Steals all his widow's toil had won;
Plunders God's world of beauty; rends away
All safety from the night, all comfort from the day.

"Then wisely is my soul elate,
    That strife should vanish, battle cease;
I'm poor, and of a low estate,
    The mother of the Prince of peace!
Joy rises in me, like a summer's morn;
Peace, peace on earth! the Prince of peace is born!"

The Savior Must Have Been a Docile Gentleman

EMILY DICKINSON (1830–1886)

The Savior must have been
A docile Gentleman—
To come so far so cold a Day
For little Fellowmen—

The Road to Bethlehem
Since He and I were Boys
Was leveled, but for that 'twould be
A rugged billion Miles—

Nativity

JOHN DONNE (1572–1631)

Immensity cloistered in thy dear womb,
Now leaves his well-beloved imprisonment,
There he hath made himself to his intent
Weak enough, now into our world to come;
But Oh, for thee, for him, hath th' Inn no room?
Yet lay him in this stall, and from the Orient,
Stars, and wisemen will travel to prevent
Th' effect of Herod's jealous general doom.
Seest thou, my Soul, with thy faith's eyes, how he
Which fills all place, yet none holds him, doth lie?
Was not his pity towards thee wondrous high,
That would have need to be pitied by thee?
Kiss him, and with him into Egypt go,
With his kind mother, who partakes thy woe.

Jest 'Fore Christmas

EUGENE FIELD (1850–1895)

Father calls me William, sister calls me Will,
Mother calls me Willie, but the fellers call me Bill!
Mighty glad I ain't a girl—ruther be a boy,
Without them sashes, curls, an' things that's worn by
    Fauntleroy!
Love to chawnk green apples an' go swimmin' in the lake—
Hate to take the castor-ile they give for bellyache!
'Most all the time, the whole year round, there ain't no flies
    on me,
But jest 'fore Christmas I'm as good as I kin be!

Got a yeller dog named Sport, sick him on the cat;
First thing she knows she does n't know where she is at!
Got a clipper sled, an' when us kids goes out to slide,
'Long comes the grocery cart, an' we all hook a ride!
But sometimes when the grocery man is worrited an' cross,
He reaches at us with his whip, an' larrups up his hoss,
An' then I laff an' holler, "Oh, ye never teched *me*!"
But jest 'fore Christmas I'm as good as I kin be!

Gran'ma says she hopes that when I git to be a man,
I'll be a missionarer like her oldest brother, Dan,
As was et up by the cannibuls that lives in Ceylon's Isle,
Where every prospeck pleases, an' only man is vile!
But gran'ma she has never been to see a Wild West show,
Nor read the Life of Daniel Boone, or else I guess she'd
    know
That Buff'lo Bill an' cowboys is good enough for me!
Excep' jest 'fore Christmas, when I'm good as I kin be!

And then old Sport he hangs around, so solemnlike an'
    still,
His eyes they seem a-sayin': "What's the matter, little Bill?"
The old cat sneaks down off her perch an' wonders what's
    become

Of them two enemies of hern that used to make things
    hum!
But I am so perlite an' tend so earnestly to biz,
That mother says to father: "How improved our Willie is!"
But father, havin' been a boy hisself, suspicions me
When, jest 'fore Christmas, I'm as good as I kin be!

For Christmas, with its lots an' lots of candies, cakes, an'
    toys,
Was made, they say, for proper kids an' not for naughty
    boys;
So wash yer face an' bresh yer hair, an' mind yer p's and
    q's,
An' don't bust out yer pantaloons, and don't wear out yer
    shoes;
Say "Yessum" to the ladies, and "Yessur" to the men,
An' when they's company, don't pass yer plate for pie
    again;
But, thinkin' of the things yer'd like to see upon that tree,
Jest 'fore Christmas be as good as yer kin be!

Carol of the Field Mice
From *The Wind in the Willows*

KENNETH GRAHAME (1859–1932)

Villagers all, this frosty tide,
Let your doors swing open wide,
Though wind may follow, and snow beside,
Yet draw us in by your fire to bide;
   Joy shall be yours in the morning!

Here we stand in the cold and the sleet,
Blowing fingers and stamping feet,
Come from far away you to greet—
you by the fire and we in the street—
   Bidding you joy in the morning!

For ere one half of the night was gone,
Sudden a star has led us on,
Raining bliss and benison—
Bliss tomorrow and more anon,
   Joy for every morning!

Goodman Joseph toiled through the snow—
Saw the star o'er a stable low;
Mary she might not further go—
Welcome thatch, and litter below!
   Joy was hers in the morning!

And then they heard the angels tell
"Who were the first to cry Nowell?
Animals all, as it befell,
In the stable where they did dwell!
   Joy shall be theirs in the morning!"

A Friend's Greeting

EDGAR A. GUEST (1881–1959)

I'd like to be the sort of friend that you have been to me;
I'd like to be the help that you've been always glad to be;
I'd like to mean as much to you each minute of the day
As you have meant, old friend of mine, to me along the
    way.

I'd like to do the big things and the splendid things for
    you,
To brush the gray from out your skies and leave them only
    blue;
I'd like to say the kindly things that I so oft have heard,
And feel that I could rouse your soul the way that mine
    you've stirred.

I'd like to give you back the joy that you have given me,
Yet that were wishing you a need I hope will never be;
I'd like to make you feel as rich as I, who travel on
Undaunted in the darkest hours with you to lean upon.

I'm wishing at this Christmas time that I could but repay
A portion of the gladness that you've strewn along my way;
And could I have one wish this year, this only would it be:
I'd like to be the sort of friend that you have been to me.

The Oxen

THOMAS HARDY (1840–1928)

Christmas Eve, and twelve of the clock.
   "Now they are all on their knees,"
An elder said as we sat in a flock
   By the embers in hearthside ease.

We pictured the meek mild creatures where
   They dwelt in their strawy pen,
Nor did it occur to one of us there
   To doubt they were kneeling then.

So fair a fancy few would weave
   In these years! Yet, I feel,
If someone said on Christmas Eve,
   "Come; see the oxen kneel

"In the lonely barton by yonder coomb
   Our childhood used to know,"
I should go with him in the gloom,
   Hoping it might be so.

Christmas (I)

GEORGE HERBERT (1593–1633)

All after pleasures as I rid one day,
   My horse and I, both tir'd, bodie and minde,
   With full crie of affections, quite astray;
I took up in the next inne I could finde.

There when I came, whom found I but my deare,
   My dearest Lord, expecting till the grief
   Of pleasures brought me to him, readie there
To be all passengers most sweet relief?

O Thou, whose glorious, yet contracted light,
   Wrapt in night's mantle, stole into a manger;
   Since my dark soul and brutish is thy right,
To Man of all beasts be not thou a stranger:

   Furnish and deck my soul, that thou mayst have
   A better lodging, than a rack, or grave.

Christmas (II)

GEORGE HERBERT (1593–1633)

The shepherds sing; and shall I silent be?
　　My God, no hymne for thee?
My soul 's a shepherd too: a flock it feeds
　　Of thoughts, and words, and deeds.
The pasture is thy word; the streams, thy grace
　　Enriching all the place.
Shepherd and flock shall sing, and all my powers
　　Out-sing the day-light houres.
Then we will chide the sunne for letting night
　　Take up his place and right:

We sing one common Lord; wherefore he should
　　Himself the candle hold.

I will go searching, till I finde a sunne
　　Shall stay, till we have done;
A willing shiner, that shall shine as gladly,
　　As frost-nipt sunnes look sadly.
Then we will sing, and shine all our own day,
　　And one another pay:
His beams shall cheer my breast, and both so twine,
Till ev'n his beams sing, and my musick shine.

Ceremonies for Christmas
ROBERT HERRICK (1591–1674)

Come, bring with a noise,
My merry, merry boys,
The Christmas Log to the firing;
While my good Dame, she
Bids ye all be free;
And drink to your heart's desiring.

With the last year's brand
Light the new block, and
For good success in his spending,
On your Psaltries play,
That sweet luck may
Come while the log is a-tinding.

Drink now the strong beer,
Cut the white loaf here,
The while the meat is a-shredding;
For the rare mince-pie
And the plums stand by
To fill the paste that's a-kneading.

Christmas-Eve, Another Ceremony
ROBERT HERRICK (1591–1674)

Come guard this night the Christmas-Pie,
That the thief, though ne'er so sly,
With his flesh-hooks, don't come nigh
        To catch it

From him, who all alone sits there,
Having his eyes still in his ear,
And a deal of nightly fear
        To watch it.

A Christmas Carol, Sung to the King in the Presence at White-Hall

ROBERT HERRICK (1591–1674)

Chorus.   What sweeter music can we bring,
Than a Carol, for to sing
The Birth of this our heavenly King?
Awake the Voice! Awake the String!
Heart, Ear, and Eye, and every thing
Awake! the while the active Finger
Runs division with the Singer.

From the Flourish they came to the Song.

Voice 1:   Dark and dull night, fly hence away,
And give the honor to this Day,
That sees December turn'd to May.

Voice 2:   If we may ask the reason, say:
The why, and wherefore all things here
Seem like the Spring-time fo the year?

Voice 3:   Why does the chilling Winter's morn
Smile, like a field beset with corn?
Or smell, like to a mead new-shorn,
Thus, on the sudden?

Voice 4:   Come and see
The cause, why things thus fragrant be:
'Tis He is born, whose quick'ning Birth
Gives life and luster, public mirth,
To Heaven and the under-Earth.

Chorus: We see Him come, and know Him ours,
Who, with His Sun-shine, and His Showers,
Turns all the patient ground to flowers.

Voice 1: The Darling of the World is come,
And fit it is, we find a room
To welcome Him.

Voice 2: The nobler part
Of all the house here, is the Heart,

Chorus: Which we will give Him; and bequeath
This Holly and this Ivy Wreath,
To do Him honor; who's our King,
And Lord of all this Revelling.

We Three Kings

JOHN HENRY HOPKINS (1820–1891)

We three kings of Orient are;
Bearing gifts we traverse afar
Field and fountain, moor and mountain,
Following yonder star:

> *O star of wonder, star of night,*
> *Star with royal beauty bright,*
> *Westward leading, still proceeding,*
> *Guide us to thy perfect light.*

Melchior.
Born a king on Bethlehem plain,
Gold I bring, to crown him again—
King for ever, ceasing never,
Over us all to reign:

Gaspar.
Frankincense to offer have I;
Incense owns a Deity nigh:
Prayer and praising, all men raising,
Worship him, God most high:

Balthazar.
Myrrh is mine; its bitter perfume
Breathes a life of gathering gloom;
Sorrowing, sighing, bleeding, dying,
Sealed in the stone-cold tomb:

All.
Glorious now, behold him arise,
King, and God, and sacrifice!
Heaven sings alleluya,
Alleluya the earth replies:

O star of wonder, star of night,
Star with royal beauty bright,
Westward leading, still proceeding,
Guide us to thy perfect light.

The Masque of Christmas
BEN JONSON (1572–1637)

Now God preserve, as you well do deserve,
    Your majesties all two there;
Your highness small, with my good lords all,
    And ladies, how do you do there?

Give me leave to ask, for I bring you a masque
    From little, little, little London;
Which say the king likes, I have passed the pikes,
    If not, old Christmas is undone.

Our dance's freight is a matter of eight,
    And two, the which are wenches:
In all they be ten, four cocks to a hen,
    And will swim to the tune like tenches.

Each hath his knight for to carry his light,
    Which some would say are torches;
To bring them here, and to lead them there,
    And home again to their own porches.

Now their intent, is above to present,
    With all the appurtenances,
A right Christmas, as of old it was,
    To be gathered out of the dances.

Which they do bring, and afore the king,
    The queen, and prince, as it were now
Drawn here by love; who over and above,
    Doth draw himself in the gear too.

Hum drum, sauce for a coney;
    No more of your martial music;
Even for the sake o' the next new stake,
    For there I do mean to use it.

And now to ye, who in place are to see,
    With roll and farthingale hoopéd:

I pray you know, though he want his bow,
   By the wings, that this is Cupid.

He might go back for to cry, What you lack?
   But that were not so witty:
His cap and coat are enough to note,
   That he is the Love o' the city.

And he leads on, though he now be gone,
   For that was only his-rule:
But now comes in, Tom of Bosoms-inn,
   And he presenteth Mis-rule.

Which you may know, by the very show,
   Albeit you never ask it:
For there you may see, what his ensigns be,
   The rope, the cheese, and the basket.

This Carol plays, and has been in his days
   A chirping boy, and a kill-pot:
Kit cobbler it is, I'm a father of his,
   And he dwells in the lane call'd Fill-pot.

But who is this? O, my daughter Cis,
   Minced-pie; with her do not dally
On pain o' your life: she's an honest cook's wife,
   And comes out of Scalding Alley.

Next in the trace, comes Gambol in place:
   And, to make my tale the shorter,
My son Hercules, ta'en out of Distaff Lane,
   But an active man, and a porter.

Now Post and Pair, old Christmas's heir,
   Doth make and a jingling sally;
And wot you who, 'tis one of my two
   Sons, card-makers in Pur Alley.

Next in a trice, with his box and his dice,
   Mac'-pipin my son, but younger,
Brings Mumming in; and the knave will win,
   For he is a costermonger.

But New Year's Gift, of himself makes shift,
    To tell you what his name is:
With orange on head, and his ginger-bread,
    Clem Wasp of Honey Lane 'tis.

This, I you tell, is our jolly Wassel,
    And for Twelfth-night more meet too:
She works by the ell, and her name is Nell,
    And she dwells in Threadneedle Street too.

Then Offering, he, with his dish and his tree,
    That in every great house keepeth,
Is by my son, young Little-worth, done,
    And in Penny-rich Street he sleepeth.

Last, Baby-cake, that an end doth make
    Of Christmas' merry, merry vein-a,
Is child Rowlan, and a straight young man,
    Though he come out of Crooked Lane-a.

There should have been, and a dozen I ween,
    But I could find but one more
Child of Christmas, and a Log it was,
    When I them all had gone o'er.

I prayéd him, in a time so trim,
    That he would make one to prance it:
And I myself would have been the twelfth,
    O but Log was too heavy to dance it.

Christmas in India

RUDYARD KIPLING (1865–1936)

Dim dawn behind the tamarisks—the sky is saffron-yellow—
As the women in the village grind the corn,
And the parrots seek the riverside, each calling to his fellow
That the Day, the staring Easter Day, is born.
Oh the white dust on the highway! Oh the stenches in the
    byway!
Oh the clammy fog that hovers over earth!
And at Home they're making merry 'neath the white and
    scarlet berry—
What part have India's exiles in their mirth?

Full day begind the tamarisks—the sky is blue and staring—
As the cattle crawl afield beneath the yoke,
And they bear One o'er the field-path, who is past all hope
    or caring,
To the ghat below the curling wreaths of smoke.
Call on Rama, going slowly, as ye bear a brother lowly—
Call on Rama—he may hear, perhaps, your voice!
With our hymn-books and our psalters we appeal to other
    altars,
And to-day we bid "good Christian men rejoice!"

High noon behind the tamarisks—the sun is hot above
    us—
As at Home the Christmas Day is breaking wan.
They will drink our healths at dinner—those who tell us
    how they love us,
And forget us till another year be gone!
Oh the toil that knows no breaking! Oh the Heimweh,
    ceaseless, aching!
Oh the black dividing Sea and alien Plain!
Youth was cheap—wherefore we sold it. Gold was good—we
    hoped to hold it,
And to-day we know the fulness of our gain.

Grey dusk behind the tamarisks—the parrots fly together—
As the sun is sinking slowly over Home;
And his last ray seems to mock us shackled in a lifelong
    tether
That drags us back how'er so far we roam.
Hard her service, poor her payment—she is ancient,
    tattered raiment—
India, she the grim Stepmother of our kind.
If a year of life be lent her, if her temple's shrine we enter,
The door is shut—we may not look behind.

Black night behind the tamarisks—the owls begin their
    chorus—
As the conches from the temple scream and bray.
With the fruitless years behind us, and the hopeless years
    before us,
Let us honor, O my brother, Christmas Day!
Call a truce, then, to our labors—let us feast with friends
    and neighbors,
And be merry as the custom of our caste;
For if "faint and forced the laughter," and if sadness follow
    after,
We are richer by one mocking Christmas past.

Eddi's Service

RUDYARD KIPLING (1865–1936)

Eddi, priest of St. Wilfrid
    In the chapel at Manhood End,
Ordered a midnight service
    For such as cared to attend.

But the Saxons were keeping Christmas,
    And the night was stormy as well.
Nobody came to service,
    Though Eddi rang the bell.

"Wicked weather for walking,"
    Said Eddi of Manhood End.
"But I must go on with the service
    For such as care to attend."

The altar-lamps were lighted,—
    An old marsh-donkey came,
Bold as a guest invited,
    And stared at the guttering flame.

The storm beat on at the windows,
    The water splashed on the floor,
And a wet, yoke-weary bullock
    Pushed in through the open door.

"How do I know what is greatest,
    How do I know what is least?
That is my Father's business,"
    Said Eddi, Wilfrid's priest.

"But—three are gathered together—
    Listen to me and attend.
I bring good news, my brethren!"
    Said Eddi, of Manhood End.

And he told the Ox of a manger,
    And a stall in Bethlehem,

And he spoke to the Ass of a Rider
    That rode to Jerusalem.

They steamed and dripped in the chancel.
    They listened and never stirred,
While, just as though they were Bishops,
    Eddi preached them The Word.

Till the gale blew off on the marshes
    And the windows showed the day.
And the Ox and the Ass together
    Wheeled and clattered away.

And when the Saxons mocked him.
    Said Eddi of Manhood End,
"I dare not shut His chapel
    On such as care to attend."

A Nativity

RUDYARD KIPLING (1865–1936)

The Babe was laid in the Manger
  Between the gentle kine—
All safe from cold and danger—
  "But it was not so with mine,
        (With mine! With mine!)
"Is it well with the child, is it well?"
  The waiting mother prayed.
"For I know not how he fell,
  And I know not where he is laid."

A Star stood forth in Heaven;
  The Watchers ran to see
The Sign of the Promise given—
  "But there comes no sign to me.
        (To me! To me!)
"*My* child died in the dark.
  Is it well with the child, is it well?
There was none to tend him or mark,
  And I know not how he fell."

The Cross was raised on high;
  The Mother grieved beside—
"But the Mother saw Him die
  And took Him when He died.
        (He died! He died!)
"Seemly and undefiled
  His burial-place was made—
Is it well, is it well with the child?
  For I know not where he is laid."

On the dawning of Easter Day
  Comes Mary Magdalene;
But the Stone was rolled away,
  And the Body was not within—
        (Within! Within!)

"Ah, who will answer my word?"
   The broken mother prayed.
"They have taken away my Lord,
   And I know not where He is Laid."

"The Star stands forth in Heaven.
   The watchers watch in vain
For Sign of the Promise given
   Of peace on Earth again—
            (Again! Again!)
"But I know for Whom he fell"—
   The steadfast mother smiled,
"Is it well with the child—is it well?
   It is well—it is well with the child!"

Christmas Bells

HENRY WADSWORTH LONGFELLOW (1807–1882)

I heard the bells on Christmas Day
Their old, familiar carols play,
   And wild and sweet
   The words repeat
Of peace on earth, good-will to men!

And thought how, as the day had come,
The belfries of all Christendom
   Had rolled along
   The unbroken song
Of peace on earth, good-will to men!

Till, ringing, singing on its way,
The world revolved from night to day,
   A voice, a chime
   A chant sublime
Of peace on earth, good-will to men!

Then from each black, accursed mouth
The cannon thundered in the South,
   And with the sound
   The carols drowned
Of peace on earth, good-will to men!

It was as if an earthquake rent
The hearth-stones of a continent,
   And made forlorn
   The households born
Of peace on earth, good-will to men!

And in despair I bowed my head;
"There is no peace on earth," I said;
   "For hate is strong,
   And mocks the song
Of peace on earth, good-will to men!"

Then pealed the bells more loud and deep:
"God is not dead; nor doth he sleep!
   The Wrong shall fail,
   The Right prevail,
With peace on earth, good-will to men!"

The Three Kings

HENRY WADSWORTH LONGFELLOW (1807–1882)

Three Kings came riding from far away,
 Melchior and Gaspar and Baltasar;
Three Wise Men out of the East were they,
And they travelled by night and they slept by day,
 For their guide was a beautiful, wonderful star.

The star was so beautiful, large, and clear,
 That all the other stars of the sky
Became a white mist in the atmosphere,
And by this they knew that the coming was near
 Of the Prince foretold in the prophecy.

Three caskets they bore on their saddle-bows,
 Three caskets of gold with golden keys;
Their robes were of crimson silk with rows
Of bells and pomegranates and furbelows,
 Their turbans like blossoming almond-trees.

And so the Three Kings rode into the West,
 Through the dusk of night, over hill and dell,
And sometimes they nodded with beard on breast,
And sometimes talked, as they paused to rest,
 With the people they met at some wayside well.

"Of the child that is born," said Baltasar,
 "Good people, I pray you, tell us the news;
For we in the East have seen his star,
And have ridden fast, and have ridden far,
 To find and worship the King of the Jews."

And the people answered, "You ask in vain;
 We know of no king but Herod the Great!"
They thought the Wise Men were men insane,
As they spurred their horses across the plain,
 Like riders in haste, and who cannot wait.

And when they came to Jerusalem,
  Herod the Great, who had heard this thing,
Sent for the Wise Men and questioned them;
And said, "Go down unto Bethlehem,
  And bring me tidings of this new king."

So they rode away; and the star stood still,
  The only one in the gray of morn;
Yes, it stopped,—it stood still of its own free will,
Right over Bethlehem on the hill,
  The city of David, where Christ was born.

And the Three Kings rode through the gate and the guard,
  Through the silent street, till their horses turned
And neighed as they entered the great inn-yard;
But the windows were closed, and the doors were barred,
  And only a light in the stable burned.

And cradled there in the scented hay,
  In the air made sweet by the breath of kine,
The little child in the manger lay,
The child, that would be king one day
  Of a kingdom not human but divine.

His mother Mary of Nazareth
  Sat watching beside his place of rest,
Watching the even flow of his breath,
For the joy of life and the terror of death
  Were mingled together in her breast.

They laid their offerings at his feet:
  The gold was their tribute to a King,
The frankincense, with its odor sweet,
Was for the Priest, the Paraclete,
  The myrhh for the body's burying.

And the mother wondered and bowed her head,
  And sat as still as a statue of stone;
Her heart was troubled yet comforted,
Remembering what the Angel had said
  Of an endless reign and of David's throne.

Then the Kings rode out of the city gate,
   With a clatter of hoofs in proud array;
But they went not back to Herod the Great
For they knew his malice and feared his hate,
   And returned to their homes by another way.

From Heaven Above to Earth I Come
MARTIN LUTHER (1483–1546)
Translated by Catherine Winkworth (1827–1878)

From heaven above to earth I come
To bear good news to every home;
Glad tidings of great joy I bring,
Whereof I now will say and sing:

To you this night is born a child
Of Mary, chosen virgin mild;
This little child, of lowly birth,
Shall be the joy of all the earth.

This is the Christ, our God and Lord,
Who in all need shall aid afford;
He will Himself your Savior be
From all your sins to set you free.

He will on you the gifts bestow
Prepared by God for all below,
That in His kingdom, bright and fair,
You may with us His glory share.

These are the tokens ye shall mark:
The swaddling-clothes and manger dark;
There ye shall find the Infant laid
By whom the heavens and earth were made."

Now let us all with gladsome cheer
Go with the shepherds and draw near
To see the precious gift of God,
Who hath His own dear Son bestowed.

Give heed, my heart, lift up thine eyes!
What is it in yon manger lies?
Who is this child, so young and fair?
The blessed Christ-child lieth there.

Welcome to earth, Thou noble Guest,
Through whom the sinful world is blest!
Thou com'st to share my misery;
What thanks shall I return to Thee?

Ah, Lord, who hast created all,
How weak art Thou, how poor and small,
That Thou dost choose Thine infant bed
Where humble cattle lately fed!

Were earth a thousand times as fair,
Beset with gold and jewels rare,
It yet were far too poor to be
A narrow cradle, Lord, for Thee.

For velvets soft and silken stuff
Thou hast but hay and straw so rough,
Whereon Thou, King, so rich and great,
As 'twere Thy heaven, art throned in state.

And thus, dear Lord, it pleaseth Thee
To make this truth quite plain to me,
That all the world's wealth, honor, might,
Are naught and worthless in Thy sight.

Ah, dearest Jesus, holy Child,
Make Thee a bed, soft, undefiled,
Within my heart, that it may be
A quiet chamber kept for Thee.

My heart for very joy doth leap,
My lips no more can silence keep;
I, too, must sing with joyful tongue
That sweetest ancient cradle-song:

Glory to God in highest heaven,
Who unto us His Son hath given!
While angels sing with pious mirth
A glad new year to all the earth.

On the Morning of Christ's Nativity
JOHN MILTON (1608–1674)

This is the Month, and this the happy morn
Wherin the Son of Heav'ns eternal King,
Of wedded Maid, and Virgin Mother born,
Our great redemption from above did bring;
For so the holy sages once did sing,
   That he our deadly forfeit should release,
And with his Father work us a perpetual peace.

That glorious Form, that Light unsufferable,
And that far-beaming blaze of Majesty,
Wherwith he wont at Heav'ns high Councel-Table,
To sit the midst of Trinal Unity,
He laid aside; and here with us to be,
   Forsook the Courts of everlasting Day,
And chose with us a darksom House of mortal Clay.

Say Heav'nly Muse, shall not thy sacred vein
Afford a present to the Infant God?
Hast thou no verse, no hymn, or solemn strein,
To welcom him to this his new abode,
Now while the Heav'n by the Suns team untrod,
   Hath took no print of the approaching light,
And all the spangled host keep watch in squadrons bright?

See how from far upon the Eastern rode
The Star-led Wisards haste with odours sweet,
O run, prevent them with thy humble ode,
And lay it lowly at his blessed feet;
Have thou the honour first, thy Lord to greet,
   And joyn thy voice unto the Angel Quire,
From out his secret Altar toucht with hallow'd fire.

The Hymn

It was the Winter wilde,
While the Heav'n-born-childe,

All meanly wrapt in the rude manger lies;
Nature in aw to him
Had doff't her gawdy trim,
　With her great Master so to sympathize:
It was no season then for her
To wanton with the Sun her lusty Paramour.

Only with speeches fair
She woo's the gentle Air
　To hide her guilty front with innocent Snow,
And on her naked shame,
Pollute with sinfull blame,
　The Saintly Vail of Maiden white to throw,
Confounded, that her Makers eyes
Should look so neer upon her foul deformities.

But he her fears to cease,
Sent down the meek-eyd Peace,
　She crown'd with Olive green, came softly sliding
Down through the turning sphear
His ready Harbinger,
　With Turtle wing the amorous clouds dividing,
And waving wide her mirtle wand,
She strikes a universall Peace through Sea and Land.

No War, or Battails sound
Was heard the World around,
　The idle spear and shield were high up hung;
The hooked Chariot stood
Unstain'd with hostile blood,
　The Trumpet spake not to the armed throng,
And Kings sate still with awfull eye,
As if they surely knew their sovran Lord was by.

But peacefull was the night
Wherin the Prince of light
　His raign of peace upon the earth began:
The Windes with wonder whist,
Smoothly the waters kist,
　Whispering new joyes to the milde Ocean,

Who now hath quite forgot to rave,
While Birds of Calm sit brooding on the charmed wave.

The Stars with deep amaze
Stand fixt in stedfast gaze,
    Bending one way their pretious influence,
And will not take their flight,
For all the morning light,
    Or *Lucifer* that often warn'd them thence;
But in their glimmering Orbs did glow,
Untill their Lord himself bespake, and bid them go.

And though the shady gloom
Had given day her room,
    The Sun himself with-held his wonted speed,
And hid his head for shame,
As his inferiour flame,
    The new enlightn'd world no more should need;
He saw a greater Sun appear
Than his bright Throne, or burning Axletree could bear.

The Shepherds on the Lawn,
Or ere the point of dawn,
    Sate simply chatting in a rustick row;
Full little thought they than,
That the mighty *Pan*
    Was kindly com to live with them below;
Perhaps their loves, or els their sheep,
Was all that did their silly thoughts so busie keep.

When such musick sweet
Their hearts and ears did greet,
    As never was by mortall finger strook,
Divinely-warbled voice
Answering the stringed noise,
    As all their souls in blisfull rapture took:
The Air such pleasure loth to lose,
With thousand echo's still prolongs each heav'nly close.

Nature that heard such sound
Beneath the hollow round

Of *Cynthia's* seat, the Airy region thrilling,
Now was almost won
To think her part was don,
   And that her raign had here its last fulfilling;
She knew such harmony alone
Could hold all Heav'n and Earth in happier union.

At last surrounds their sight
A Globe of circular light,
   That with long beams the shame-fac't night array'd,
The helmed Cherubim
And sworded Seraphim,
   Are seen in glittering ranks with wings displaid,
Harping in loud and solemn quire,
With unexpressive notes to Heav'ns new-born Heir.

Such Musick (as 'tis said)
Before was never made,
   But when of old the sons of morning sung,
While the Creator Great
His constellations set,
   And the well-ballanc't world on hinges hung,
And cast the dark foundations deep,
And bid the weltring waves their oozy channel keep.

Ring out ye Crystall sphears,
Once bless our human ears,
   (If ye have power to touch our senses so)
And let your silver chime
Move in melodious time;
   And let the Base of Heav'ns deep Organ blow,
And with your ninefold harmony
Make up full consort to th' Angelike symphony.

For if such holy Song
Enwrap our fancy long,
   Time will run back, and fetch the age of gold,
And speckl'd vanity
Will sicken soon and die,
   And leprous sin will melt from earthly mould,

And Hell it self will pass away,
And leave her dolorous mansions to the peering day.

Yea Truth, and Justice then
Will down return to men,
   Th' enameld *Arras* of the Rain-bow wearing,
And Mercy set between,
Thron'd in Celestiall sheen,
   With radiant feet the tissued clouds down stearing,
And Heav'n as at som festivall,
Will open wide the Gates of her high Palace Hall.

But wisest Fate sayes no,
This must not yet be so,
   The Babe lies yet in smiling Infancy,
That on the bitter cross
Must redeem our loss;
   So both himself and us to glorifie:
Yet first to those ychain'd in sleep,
The wakefull trump of doom must thunder through the
     deep,

With such a horrid clang
As on mount *Sinai* rang
   While the red fire, and smouldring clouds out brake:
The aged Earth agast
With terrour of that blast,
   Shall from the surface to the center shake;
When at the worlds last session,
The dreadfull Judge in middle Air shall spread his throne.

And then at last our bliss
Full and perfect is,
   But now begins; for from this happy day
Th' old Dragon under ground
In straiter limits bound,
   Not half so far casts his usurped sway,
And wrath to see his Kingdom fail,
Swindges the scaly Horrour of his foulded tail.

The Oracles are dumm,
No voice or hideous humm
   Runs through the arched roof in words deceiving.
Apollo from his shrine
Can no more divine,
   With hollow shreik the steep of *Delphos* leaving.
No nightly trance, or breathed spell,
Inspire's the pale-ey'd Priest from the prophetic cell.

The lonely mountains o're,
And the resounding shore,
   A voice of weeping heard, and loud lament;
From haunted spring, and dale
Edg'd with poplar pale,
   The parting Genius is with sighing sent,
With flowre-inwov'n tresses torn
The Nimphs in twilight shade of tangled thickets mourn.

In consecrated Earth,
And on the holy Hearth,
   The *Lars,* and *Lemures* moan with midnight plaint,
In Urns, and Altars round,
A drear, and dying sound
   Affrights the *Flamins* at their service quaint;
And the chill Marble seems to sweat,
While each peculiar power forgoes his wonted seat.

Peor, and *Baalim,*
Forsake their Temples dim,
   With that twice-batter'd god of *Palestine,*
And mooned *Ashtaroth,*
Heav'ns Queen and Mother both,
   Now sits not girt with Tapers holy shine,
The Libyc *Hammon* shrinks his horn,
In vain the *Tyrian* Maids their wounded *Thamuz* mourn.

And sullen *Moloch* fled,
Hath left in shadows dred,
   His burning Idol all of blackest hue,
In vain with Cymbals ring,

They call the grisly king,
  In dismall dance about the furnace blue;
The brutish gods of *Nile* as fast,
Isis and *Orus,* and the Dog *Anubis* hast.

Nor is *Osiris* seen
In *Memphian* Grove, or Green,
  Trampling the unshowr'd Grasse with lowings loud:
Nor can he be at rest
Within his sacred chest,
  Naught but profoundest Hell can be his shroud,
In vain with Timbrel'd Anthems dark
The sable-stoled Sorcerers bear his worshipt Ark.

He feels from *Juda's* Land
The dredded Infants hand,
  The rayes of *Bethlehem* blind his dusky eyn;
Nor all the gods beside,
Longer dare abide,
  Not *Typhon* huge ending in snaky twine:
Our Babe to shew his Godhead true,
Can in his swadling bands controul the damned crew.

So when the Sun in bed,
Curtain'd with cloudy red,
  Pillows his chin upon an Orient wave,
The flocking shadows pale,
Troop to th' infernall jail,
  Each fetter'd Ghost slips to his severall grave,
And the yellow-skirted *Fayes,*
Fly after the Night-steeds, leaving their Moon-lov'd maze.

But see the Virgin blest,
Hath laid her Babe to rest.
  Time is our tedious Song should here have ending,
Heav'ns youngest teemed Star,
Hath fixt her polisht Car,
  Her sleeping Lord with Handmaid Lamp attending:
And all about the Courtly Stable,
Bright-harnest Angels sit in order serviceable.

Silent Night

JOSEPH MOHR (1792–1848)

Silent night, holy night,
All is calm, all is bright
Round yon virgin mother and child.
Holy infant, so tender and mild,
Sleep in heavenly peace.
Sleep in heavenly peace.

Silent night, holy night,
Shepherds quake at the sight,
Glories stream from heaven afar,
Heavenly hosts sing alleluia;
Christ, the Savior, is born!
Christ, the Savior, is born!

Silent night, holy night,
Son of God, love's pure light
Radiant beams from thy holy face,
With the dawn of redeeming grace,
Jesus, Lord, at thy birth.
Jesus, Lord, at thy birth.

A Visit from St. Nicholas

Generally attributed to
CLEMENT CLARKE MOORE (1779–1863)

'Twas the night before Christmas,
   when all through the house
Not a creature was stirring,
   not even a mouse;
The stockings were hung
   by the chimney with care,
In hopes that St. Nicholas
   soon would be there;

The children were nestled
   all snug in their beds,
While visions of sugar-plums
   danced through their heads;
And Mamma in her kerchief,
   and I in my cap,
Had just settled our brains
   for a long winter's nap,

When out on the lawn
   there arose such a clatter,
I sprang from my bed
   to see what was the matter.
Away to the window
   I flew like a flash,
Tore open the shutters
   and threw up the sash.

The moon on the breast
   of the new-fallen snow
Gave a lustre of mid-day
   to objects below,
When, what to my wondering
   eyes did appear,
But a miniature sleigh,
   and eight tiny rein-deer,

With a little old driver
   so lively and quick,
I knew in a moment
   he must be St. Nick.
More rapid than eagles
   his coursers they came,
And he whistled, and shouted,
   and called them by name:

"Now, Dasher! now, Dancer!
   now, Prancer and Vixen!
On, Comet! on, Cupid!
   on, Donder and Blixen!
To the top of the porch!
   to the top of the wall!
Now dash away! dash away!
   dash away, all!"

As leaves that before
   the wild hurricane fly,
When they meet with an obstacle,
   mount to the sky,
So up to the house-top
   the coursers they flew,
With the sleigh full of toys,
   and St. Nicholas too—

And then in a twinkling,
   I heard on the roof
The prancing and pawing
   of each little hoof.
As I drew in my head,
   and was turning around,
Down the chimney St. Nicholas
   came with a bound.

He was dressed all in fur,
   from his head to his foot,
And his clothes were all tarnished
   with ashes and soot;

A bundle of toys he had
　　flung on his back,
And he looked like a peddler
　　just opening his pack.

His eyes—how they twinkled!
　　his dimples, how merry!
His cheeks were like roses,
　　his nose like a cherry!
His droll little mouth
　　was drawn up like a bow,
And the beard on his chin
　　was as white as the snow;

The stump of a pipe
　　he held tight in his teeth,
And the smoke it encircled
　　his head like a wreath;
He had a broad face
　　and a round little belly
That shook when he laughed,
　　like a bowl full of jelly.

He was chubby and plump,
　　a right jolly old elf,
And I laughed when I saw him
　　in spite of myself;
A wink of his eye and
　　a twist of his head
Soon gave me to know
　　I had nothing to dread;

He spoke not a word, but
　　went straight to his work,
And filled all the stockings;
　　then turned with a jerk,
And laying his finger
　　aside of his nose,
And giving a nod, up the
　　chimney he rose.

He sprang to his sleigh,
    to his team gave a whistle,
And away they all flew
    like the down of a thistle.
But I heard him exclaim
    ere he drove out of sight—

"HAPPY CHRISTMAS
        TO ALL
    AND TO ALL
        A GOOD NIGHT!"

French Noel

WILLIAM MORRIS (1834–1896)

Masters, in this Hall,
    Hear ye news to-day
Brought from over sea,
    And ever I you pray.

Nowell! Nowell! Nowell! Nowell sing we clear
Holpen are all folk on earth, Born is God's Son so dear:
Nowell! Nowell! Nowell! Nowell sing we loud!
God to-day hath poor folk rais'd, And cast down the proud.

    Going over the hills,
        Through the milk-white snow,
    Heard I ewes bleat
        While the wind did blow.

    Shepherds many an one
        Sat among the sheep,
    No man spake more word
        Than they had been asleep.

    Quoth I "Fellows mine,
        Why this guise sit ye?
    Making but dull cheer,
        Shepherds though ye be?

    "Shepherds should of right
        Leap and dance and sing;
    Thus to see ye sit
        Is a right strange thing."

    Quoth these fellows then,
        "To Bethlem town we go,
    To see a mighty Lord
        Lie in a manger low."

    "How name ye this Lord,
        Shepherds?" then said I.

"Very *God*," they said,
  "Come from Heaven high."

Then to Bethlem town
  We went two and two
And in a sorry place
  Heard the oxen low.

Therein did we see
  A sweet and goodly May
And a fair old man;
  Upon the straw She lay.

And a little Child
  On Her arm had She;
"Wot ye Who this is?"
  Said the hinds to me.

Ox and ass Him know,
  Kneeling on their knee:
Wondrous joy had I
  This little Babe to see.

This is Christ the Lord
  Masters, be ye glad!
Christmas is come in,
  And no folk should be sad.

Nowell! Nowell! Nowell! Nowell sing we clear
Holpen are all folk on earth, Born is God's Son so dear:
Nowell! Nowell! Nowell! Nowell sing we loud!
God to-day hath poor folk rais'd, And cast down the proud.

Good King Wenceslas

J. M. NEALE (1818–1866)

Good King Wenceslas looked out,
 On the Feast of Stephen,
When the snow lay round about,
 Deep, and crisp, and even:
Brightly shone the moon that night,
 Though the frost was cruel,
When a poor man came in sight,
 Gathering winter fuel.

"Hither, page, and stand by me,
 If thou know'st it, telling,
Yonder peasant, who is he?
 Where and what his dwelling?"
"Sire, he lives a good league hence,
 Underneath the mountain,
Right against the forest fence,
 By Saint Agnes' fountain."

"Bring me flesh, and bring me wine,
 Bring me pine-logs hither:
Thou and I will see him dine,
 When we bear them thither."
Page and monarch, forth they went,
 Forth they went together;
Through the rude wind's wild lament
 And the bitter weather.

"Sire, the night is darker now,
 And the wind blows stronger;
Fails my heart, I know not how;
 I can go no longer."
"Mark my footsteps, good my page;
 Tread thou in them boldly:
Thou shalt find the winter's rage
 Freeze thy blood less coldly."

In his master's steps he trod,
  Where the snow lay dinted;
Heat was in the very sod
  Which the Saint had printed.
Therefore, Christian men, be sure,
  Wealth or rank possessing,
Ye who now will bless the poor,
  Shall yourselves find blessing.

"Hear the sledges with the bells"
(First stanza of "The Bells")

EDGAR ALLAN POE (1809–1849)

Hear the sledges with the bells—
    Silver bells!
What a world of merriment their melody foretells!
How they tinkle, tinkle, tinkle,
  In the icy air of night!
While the stars, that oversprinkle
All the heavens, seem to twinkle
  With a crystalline delight
Keeping time, time, time,
  In a sort of Runic rhyme.
To the tintinnabulation that so musically wells
From the bells, bells, bells, bells,
  Bells, bells, bells—
From the jingling and the tinkling of the bells.

A Christmas Carol

CHRISTINA ROSSETTI (1830–1894)

Before the paling of the stars,
  Before the winter morn,
  Before the earliest cock-crow
Jesus Christ was born:
    Born in a stable,
  Cradled in a manger,
In the world His hands had made
    Born a stranger.

Priest and King lay fast asleep
  In Jerusalem,
Young and old lay fast asleep
  In crowded Bethlehem:
Saint and Angel, ox and ass,
    Kept a watch together,
  Before the Christmas daybreak
  In the winter weather.

Jesus on his Mother's breast
  In the stable cold,
Spotless Lamb of God was He,
  Shepherd of the fold:
Let us kneel with Mary Maid,
  With Joseph bent and hoary,
With Saint and Angel, ox and ass,
  To hail the King of Glory.

What Can I Give Him?

CHRISTINA ROSSETTI (1830–1894)

What can I give Him
   Poor as I am?
If I were a shepherd
   I would bring a lamb,
If I were a Wise Man,
   I would do my part,—
Yet what I can I give Him,
   Give my heart.

"Heap on more wood!"
(From the Introduction to Canto Sixth, "Marmion")

Sir Walter Scott (1771–1832)

Heap on more wood!—the wind is chill;
But let it whistle as it will,
We'll keep our Christmas merry still.
Each age has deemed the new-born year
The fittest time for festal cheer.
Even heathen yet, the savage Dane
At Iol more deep the mead did drain;
High on the beach his galley drew,
And feasted all his pirate crew;
Then in his low and pine-built hall,
Where shields and axes decked the wall,
They gorged upon the half-dressed steer;
Caroused in seas of sable beer;
While round, in brutal jest, were thrown
The half-gnawed rib and marrow-bone,
Or listened all, in grim delight,
While scalds yelled out the joy of fight,
Then forth in frenzy would they hie,
While wildly loose their red locks fly;
And, dancing round the blazing pile,
They make such barbarous mirth the while,
As best might to the mind recall
The boisterous joys of Odin's hall.
And well our Christian sire of old
Loved when the year its course had rolled,
And brought blithe Christmas back again,
With all his hospitable train.
Domestic and religious rite
Gave honour to the holy night:
On Christmas eve the bells were rung;
On Christmas eve the mass was sung;
That only night, in all the year,

Saw the stoled priest the chalice rear.
The damsel donned her kirtle sheen;
The hall was dressed with holly green;
Forth to the wood did merry men go,
To gather in the mistletoe;
Then opened wide the baron's hall
To vassal, tenant, serf, and all;
Power laid his rod of rule aside,
And ceremony doffed his pride.
The heir, with roses in his shoes,
That night might village partner choose;
The lord, underogating, share
The vulgar game of "post and pair."
All hailed, with uncontrolled delight,
And general voice, the happy night
That to the cottage, as the crown,
Brought tidings of salvation down.
The fire, with well-dried logs supplied,
Went roaring up the chimney wide;
The huge hall-table's oaken face,
Scrubbed till it shone, the day to grace,
Bore then upon its massive board
No mark to part the squire and lord.
Then was brought in the lusty brawn
By old blue-coated serving man;
Then the grim boar's head frowned on high,
Crested with bays and rosemary.
Well can the green-garbed ranger tell,
How, when, and where the monster fell;
What dogs before his death he tore,
And all the baiting of the boar.
The Wassail round, in good brown bowls,
Garnished with ribbons, blithely trowls.
There the huge sirloin reeked; hard by
Plum-porridge stood, and Christmas pie;
Nor failed old Scotland to produce,
At such high tide, her savoury goose.
Then came the merry masquers in,

And carols roared with blithesome din;
If unmelodious was the song,
It was a hearty note, and strong,
Who lists may in their mumming see
Traces of ancient mystery;
White shirts supplied the masquerade,
And smutted cheeks the vizors made:
But, what masquers, richly dight,
Can boast of bosoms half so light?
England was merry England, when
Old Christmas brought his sports again.
'Twas Christmas broached the mightiest ale;
'Twas Christmas told the merriest tale;
A Christmas gambol oft could cheer
The poor man's heart through half the year.

It Came Upon the Midnight Clear
EDMUND HAMILTON SEARS (1810–1876)

It came upon the midnight clear,
That glorious song of old,
From angels bending near the earth
To touch their harps of gold:
"Peace on the earth, good will to men,
From heaven's all gracious King."
The world in solemn stillness lay
To hear the angels sing.

Still through the cloven skies they come
With peaceful wings unfurled,
And still their heavenly music floats
O'er all the weary world;
Above its sad and lowly plains
They bend on hovering wing,
And ever o'er its Babel-sounds
The blessed angels sing.

Yet with the woes of sin and strife
The world has suffered long;
Beneath the heavenly hymn have rolled
Two thousand years of wrong;
And warring humankind hears not
The tidings which they bring.
O hush the noise and cease your strife
And hear the angels sing.

For lo! The days are hastening on,
By prophets seen of old,
When with the ever-circling years
Shall come the time foretold,
When peace shall over all the earth
Its ancient splendors fling,
And all the world give back the song
Which now the angels sing.

The Nativity of Our Lord and Saviour Jesus Christ

Christopher Smart (1722–1771)

Where is this stupendous stranger?
  Swains of Solyma, advise;
Lead me to my Master's manger,
  Shew me where my Saviour lies.

O Most Mighty! O Most Holy!
  Far beyond the seraph's thought,
Art thou then so mean and lowly
  As unheeded prophets taught?

O the magnitude of meekness!
  Worth from worth immortal sprung;
O the strength of infant weakness,
  If eternal is so young!

If so young and thus eternal,
  Michael tune the shepherd's reed,
Where the scenes are ever vernal,
  And the loves be love indeed!

See the God blasphem'd and doubted
  In the schools of Greece and Rome;
See the pow'rs of darkness routed,
  Taken at their utmost gloom.

Nature's decorations glisten
  Far above their usual trim;
Birds on box and laurels listen,
  As so near the cherubs hymn.

Boreas now no longer winters
  On the desolated coast;
Oaks no more are riv'n in splinters
  By the whirlwind and his host.

Spinks and ouzles sing sublimely,
  "We too have a Saviour born";
Whiter blossoms burst untimely
  On the blest Mosaic thorn.

God all-bounteous, all-creative,
  Whom no ills from good dissuade,
Is incarnate, and a native
  Of the very world he made.

New Prince, New Pomp
ROBERT SOUTHWELL (1561–1595)

Behold, a silly tender Babe
   In freezing winter night
In homely manger trembling lies,
   Alas, a piteous sight!

The inns are full; no man will yield
   This little pilgrim bed,
But forced he is with silly beasts
   In crib to shroud his head.

Despise him not for lying there,
   First, what he is inquire;
An orient pearl is often found
   In depth of dirty mire.

Weigh not his crib, his wooden dish,
   Nor beasts that by him feed;
Weigh not his Mother's poor attire,
   Nor Joseph's simple weed.

This stable is a Prince's court,
   This crib his chair of state;
The beasts are parcel of his pomp,
   The wooden dish his plate.

The persons in that poor attire
   His royal liveries wear;
The Prince himself is come from heaven;
   This pomp is prized there.

With joy approach, O Christian wight,
   Do homage to thy King;
And highly praise his humble pomp,
   Which he from heaven doth bring.

The Burning Babe
ROBERT SOUTHWELL (1561–1595)

As I in hoary Winter's night stood shiveringe in the snowe,
Surpris'd I was with sodayne heat, which made my hart to
glowe;
And lifting upp a fearfull eye to vewe what fire was nere,
A prety Babe all burninge bright, did in the ayre appeare,
Who scorchèd with excessive heate, such floodes of teares
did shedd,
As though His floodes should quench His flames which
with His teares were fedd;
Alas! quoth He, but newly borne, in fiery heates I frye,
Yet none approach to warme their hartes or feele my fire
but I!
My faultles brest the fornace is, the fuell woundinge
thornes,
Love is the fire, and sighes the smoke, the ashes shame and
scornes;
The fuell Justice layeth on, and Mercy blowes the coales,
The mettall in this fornace wrought are men's defilèd
soules,
For which, as nowe on fire I am, to worke them to their
good,
So will I melt into a bath to washe them in My bloode:
With this He vanisht out of sight, and swiftly shroncke
awaye,
And straight I callèd unto mynde that it was Christmas-
daye.

Christmas at Sea

ROBERT LOUIS STEVENSON (1850–1894)

The sheets were frozen hard, and they cut the naked hand;
The decks were like a slide, where a seaman scarce could
    stand;
The wind was a nor'wester, blowing squally off the sea;
And cliffs and spouting breakers were the only things a-lee.

They heard the surf a-roaring before the break of day;
But 'twas only with the peep of light we saw how ill we lay.
We tumbled every hand on deck instanter, with a shout,
And we gave her the maintops'l, and stood by to go about.
All day we tacked and tacked between the South Head and
    the North;
All day we hauled the frozen sheets, and got no further
    forth;
All day as cold as charity, in bitter pain and dread,
For very life and nature we tacked from head to head.

We gave the South a wider berth, for there the tide-race
    roared;
But every tack we made we brought the North Head close
    aboard;
So 's we saw the cliffs and houses, and the breakers running
    high,
And the coastguard in his garden, with his glass against his
    eye.

The frost was on the village roofs as white as ocean foam;
The good red fires were burning bright in every 'longshore
    home;
The windows sparkled clear, and the chimneys volleyed out;
And I vow we sniffed the victuals as the vessel went about.

The bells upon the church were rung with a mighty jovial
    cheer;

For it's just that I should tell you how (of all days in the
    year)
This day of our adversity was blessèd Christmas morn,
And the house above the coastguard's was the house where
    I was born.

O well I saw the pleasant room, the pleasant faces there,
My mother's silver spectacles, my father's silver hair;
And well I saw the firelight, like a flight of homely elves,
Go dancing round the china-plates that stand upon the
    shelves.

And well I knew the talk they had, the talk that was of me,
Of the shadow on the household and the son that went to
    sea;
And O the wicked fool I seemed, in every kind of way,
To be here and hauling frozen ropes on blessèd Christmas
    Day.

They lit the high sea-light, and the dark began to fall.
"All hands to loose topgallant sails," I heard the captain
    call.
"By the Lord, she'll never stand it," our first mate, Jackson,
    cried.
. . . "It's the one way or the other, Mr. Jackson," he replied.

She staggered to her bearings, but the sails were new and
    good,
And the ship smelt up to windward just as though she
    understood.
As the winter's day was ending, in the entry of the night,
We cleared the weary headland, and passed below the light.

And they heaved a mighty breath, every soul on board but
    me,
As they saw her nose again pointing handsome out to sea;
But all that I could think of, in the darkness and the cold,
Was just that I was leaving home and my folks were growing
    old.

Sleep, Baby, Sleep!
JOHN ADDINGTON SYMONDS (1840–1893)

Sleep, baby, sleep! the Mother sings:
Heaven's angels kneel and fold their wings.
Sleep, baby, sleep!

With swathes of scented hay thy bed
By Mary's hand at eve was spread.
Sleep, baby, sleep!

At midnight came the shepherds, they
Whom seraphs wakened by the way.
Sleep, baby, sleep!

And three kings from the East afar
Ere dawn came guided by a star.
Sleep, baby, sleep!

They brought thee gifts of gold and gems
Rich orient pearls, pure diadems.
Sleep, baby, sleep!

But thou who liest slumbering there
Art King of kings, earth, ocean, air.
Sleep, baby, sleep!

Sleep, baby, sleep! the shepherds sing:
Through heaven, through earth, hosannas ring
Sleep, baby, sleep!

While Shepherds Watched Their Flocks by Night

NAHUM TATE (1652–1715)

While shepherds watched their flocks by night,
   All seated on the ground,
The angel of the Lord came down,
   And glory shone around.

Fear not! said he; for mighty dread
   Had seized their troubled mind:
Glad tidings of great joy I bring
   To you and all mankind.

To you, in David's town, this day
   Is born, of David's line,
A Saviour, who is Christ the Lord;
   And this shall be the sign:

The heavenly Babe you there shall find
   To human view displayed,
All meanly wrapped in swaddling bands
   And in a manger laid.

Thus spake the seraph; and forthwith
   Appeared a shining throng
Of angels praising God, and thus
   Addressed their joyful song:

All glory be to God on high,
   And to the earth be peace;
Good will henceforth from heaven to men
   Begin and never cease!

Christmas and New Year Bells
ALFRED LORD TENNYSON (1809–1892)

The time draws near the birth of Christ:
   The moon is hid; the night is still;
   The Christmas bells from hill to hill
Answer each other in the mist.

Four voices of four hamlets round,
   From far and near, on mead and moor,
   Swell out and fail, as if a door
Were shut between me and the sound:

Each voice four changes on the wind,
   That now dilate, and now decrease,
   Peace and goodwill, goodwill and peace,
Peace and goodwill, to all mankind.

This year I slept and woke with pain,
   I almost wish'd no more to wake,
   And that my hold on life would break
Before I heard those bells again:

But they the troubled spirit rule,
   For they controll'd me when a boy;
   They bring me sorrow touch'd with joy,
The merry, merry bells of Yule.

Ring out, wild bells, to the wild sky,
   The flying cloud, the frosty light:
   The year is dying in the night;
Ring out, wild bells, and let him die.

Ring out the old, ring in the new,
   Ring, happy bells, across the snow:
   The year is going, let him go;
Ring out the false, ring in the true.

Ring out the grief that saps the mind,
   For those that here we see no more;

Ring out the feud of rich and poor,
Ring in redress to all mankind.

Ring out a slowly dying cause,
   And ancient forms of party strife;
   Ring in the nobler modes of life,
With sweeter manners, purer laws.

Ring out the want, the care, the sin,
   The faithless coldness of the times;
   Ring out, ring out my mournful rhymes,
But ring the fuller minstrel in.

Ring out false pride in place and blood,
   The civic slander and the spite;
   Ring in the love of truth and right,
Ring in the common love of good.

Ring out old shapes of foul disease,
   Ring out the narrowing lust of gold;
   Ring out the thousand wars of old
Ring in the thousand years of peace.

Ring in the valiant man and free,
   The larger heart, the kindlier hand;
   Ring out the darkness of the land,
Ring in the Christ that is to be.

The Mahogany Tree
WILLIAM MAKEPEACE THACKERAY (1811–1863)

Christmas is here:
Winds whistle shrill.
Icy and chill:
Little care we.
Little we fear
Weather without,
Sheltered about
The Mahogany Tree.

Commoner greens,
Ivy and oaks,
Poets, in jokes,
Sing, do you see:
Good fellows' shins
Here, boys, are found,
Twisting around
The Mahogany Tree.

Once on the boughs
Birds of rare plume
Sang, in its bloom:
Night birds are we;
Here we carouse,
Singing, like them,
Perched round the stem
Of the jolly old tree.

Here let us sport,
Boys, as we sit:
Laughter and wit
Flashing so free.
Life is but short—
When we are gone,
Let them sing on,
Round the old tree.

Evenings we knew,
Happy as this;
Faces we miss,
Pleasant to see.
Kind hearts and true,
Gentle and just,
Peace to your dust!
We sing round the tree.

Care, like a dun,
Lurks at the gate:
Let the dog wait;
Happy we'll be!
Drink every one;
Pile up the coals,
Fill the red bowls,
Round the old tree!

Drain we the cup.—
Friend, art afraid?
Spirits are laid
In the Red Sea.
Mantle it up;
Empty it yet;
Let us forget,
Round the old tree.

Sorrows, begone!
Life and its ills,
Duns and their bills,
Bid we to flee.
Come with the dawn
Blue-devil sprite,
Leave us to-night,
Round the old tree.

Jack Frost
CELIA THAXTER (1835–1894)

Rustily creak the crickets:
    Jack Frost came down last night,
He slid to the earth on a starbeam,
    keen and sparkling and bright;
He sought in the grass for the crickets
    with delicate icy spear,
So sharp and fine and fatal,
    and he stabbed them far and near.
Only a few stout fellows,
    thawed by the morning sun,
Chirrup a mournful echo
    of by-gone frolic and fun.
But yesterday such a rippling
    chorus ran all over the land,
Over the hills and the valleys,
    down to the gray sea-sand
Millions of merry harlequins,
    skipping and dancing in glee,
Cricket and locust and grasshopper,
    happy as happy could be:
Scooping rich caves in ripe apples,
    and feeding on honey and spice,
Drunk with the mellow sunshine,
    nor dreaming of spears of ice!
Was it not enough that the crickets
    your weapon of power should pierce?
Pray what have you done to the flowers?
    Jack Frost, you are cruel and fierce.
With never a sign or a whisper,
    you kissed them and lo, they exhale
Their beautiful lives; they are drooping,
    their sweet color ebbs, they are pale,

They fade and they die! See the pansies,
    yet striving so hard to unfold
Their garments of velvety splendor,
    all Tyrian purple and gold.
But how weary they look, and how withered,
    like handsome court dames, who all night
Have danced at the ball till the sunrise
    struck chill to their hearts with its light.
Where hides the wood-aster? She vanished
    as snow wreaths dissolve in the sun
The moment you touched her. Look yonder,
    where sober and gray as a nun,
The maple-tree stands that at sunset
    was blushing and red as the sky;
At its foot, glowing scarlet as fire,
    its robes of magnificence lie.
Despoiler! stripping the world
    as you strip the shivering tree
Of color and sound and perfume,
    scaring the bird and the bee,
Turning beauty to ashes—oh to join
    the swift swallows and fly
Far away out of sight of your mischief!
    I give you no welcome, not I!

Mrs. Kriss Kringle

EDITH M. THOMAS (1854–1925)

Oh, I laugh to hear what grown folk
   Tell the young folk of Kriss Kringle,
In the Northland, where unknown folk
   Love to feel the frost-wind tingle.

Yes, I laugh to hear the grown folk
   Tell you young folk how Kriss Kringle
Travels 'round the world like lone folk,
   None to talk with—always single!

Would a grim and grave old fellow
   (Not a chick nor child to care for)
Keep a heart so warm and mellow
   That all children he'd prepare for?

Do you think, my little maiden,
   He could ever guess your wishes—
That you'd find your stocking laden
   With a doll and set of dishes?

No; the truth is, some one whispers
   In the ear he hears the best with,
What to suit the youngest lispers,
   Boys and girls, and all the rest with.

Some one (ah, you guess in vain, dear!)
   Nestled close by old Kriss Kringle,
Laughs to see the prancing reindeer,
   Laughs to hear the sledge bells jingle.

Dear old lady, small and rosy!
   In the nipping, Christmas weather,
Nestled close, so warm and cozy,
   These two chat, for hours together.

So, if I were in your places,
   Rob and Hal, and Kate, and Mary,

I would be in the good graces
   Of this lovely, shy old fairy.

Still I laugh to hear the grown folk
   Tell you young folk how Kriss Kringle
Travels 'round the world, like lone folk,—
   None to talk with—always single!

The Nativity

HENRY VAUGHAN (1621–1695)

Peace? and to all the world? sure, one
And he the prince of peace, hath none.
He travels to be born, and then
Is born to travel more agen.
Poor *Galile*! thou can'st not be
The place for his Nativity.
His restless mother's call'd away,
And not deliver'd till she pay.
   A *Tax*? 'tis so still! we can see
The Church thrive in her misery;
And like her head at *Bethlem,* rise
When she opprest with troubles, lyes.
Rise? should all fall, we cannot be
In more extremities than he.
Great *Type* of passions! come what will,
Thy grief exceeds all *copies* still.
Thou cam'st from heav'n to earth, that we
Might go from Earth to Heav'n with thee.
And though thou found'st no welcom here,
Thou did'st provide us *mansions* there.
A *stable* was thy *Court,* and when
Men turn'd to *beasts*; Beasts would be *Men.*
They were thy *Courtiers,* others none;
And their poor *Manger* was thy *Throne.*
No swadling *silks* thy Limbs did fold,
Though thou could'st turn thy Rays to gold.
No *Rockers* waited on thy birth,
No *Cradles* stirr'd: nor songs of mirth;
But her chast *Lap* and sacred *Brest*
Which lodg'd thee first, did give thee *rest.*
   But stay: what light is that doth stream,
And drop here in a gilded beam?

It is thy Star runs *page,* and brings
Thy tributary *Eastern* Kings.
Lord! grant some *Light* to us, that we
May with them find the way to thee.
Behold what mists eclipse the day:
How dark it is! shed down one *Ray*
To guide us out of this sad night,
And say once more, *Let there be Light.*

The True Christmas

HENRY VAUGHAN (1621–1695)

So stick up *Ivie* and the *Bays,*
And then restore the *heathen* ways.
Green will remind you of the spring,
Though this great day denies the thing.
And mortifies the Earth and all
But your wild *Revels,* and loose *Hall.*
Could you wear *Flow'rs,* and *Roses* strow
Blushing upon your breasts *warm Snow,*
That very *dress* your lightness will
Rebuke, and wither at the Ill.
The brightness of this day we owe
Not unto *Music, Masque* nor *Showe:*
Nor gallant *furniture,* nor *Plate;*
But to the *Manger's* means Estate.
His *life* while here, as well as *birth,*
Was but a check to *pomp* and *mirth;*
And all mans *greatness* you may see
Condemn'd by his *humility.*
    Then leave your open *house* and *noise,*
To welcom him with *holy Joys,*
And the poor *Shepherd's* watchfulness:
Whom *light* and *hymns* from Heav'n did bless.
What you *abound* with, cast abroad
To those that *want,* and ease your loade.
Who empties thus, will bring more in;
But riot is both *loss* and *Sin.*
Dress finely what comes not in sight,
And then you keep your *Christmas* right.

A Christmas Carol
GEORGE WITHER (1588–1667)

So now is come our joyful feast,
   Let every man be jolly;
Each room with ivy leaves is dressed,
   And every post with holly.
     Though some churls at our mirth repine,
     Round your foreheads garlands twine,
     Drown sorrow in a cup of wine,
   And let us all be merry.

Now all our neighbors' chimnies smoke,
   And Christmas blocks are burning;
Their ovens they with baked meats choke,
   And all their spits are turning.
     Without the door let sorrow lie,
     And if for cold it hap to die,
     We'll bury it in a Christmas pie,
   And evermore be merry.

Now every lad is wondrous trim,
   And no man minds his labor;
Our lasses have provided them
   A bagpipe and a tabor.
     Young men and maids, and girls and boys,
     Give life to one another's joys;
     And you anon shall by their noise
   Perceive that they are merry.

Rank misers now do sparing shun,
   Their hall of music soundeth;
And dogs thence with whole shoulders run,
   So all things aboundeth.
     The country-folk themselves advance,
     For crowdy-mutton's come out of France;
     And Jack shall pipe and Jill shall dance,
   And all the town be merry.

Ned Swatch hath fetched his bands from pawn,
   And all his best apparel;
Brisk Nell hath bought a ruff of lawn
    With droppings of the barrel.
      And those that hardly all the year
      Had bread to eat or rags to wear,
      Will have both clothes and dainty fare,
    And all the day be merry.

Now poor men to the justices
    With capons make their errands;
And if they hap to fail of these,
    They plague them with their warrants.
      But now they feed them with good cheer,
      And what they want they take in beer,
      For Christmas comes but once a year,
    And then they shall be merry.

Good farmers in the country nurse
    The poor, that else were undone;
Some landlords spend their money worse,
    On lust and pride at London.
      There the roisters they do play,
      Drab and dice their land away,
      Which may be ours another day;
    And therefore let's be merry.

The client now his suit forbears,
    The prisoner's heart is eased;
The debtor drinks away his cares,
    And for the time is pleased.
      Though others' purses be more fat,
      Why should we pine or grieve at that;
      Hang sorrow, care will kill a cat,
    And therefore let's be merry.

Hark how the wags abroad do call
  Each other forth to rambling;
Anon you'll see them in the hall,
    For nuts and apples scrambling;
      Hark how the roofs with laughters sound,
      Anon they'll think the house goes round;
      For they the cellar's depths have found,
    And there they will be merry.

The wenches with their wassail-bowls
  About the streets are singing;
The boys are come to catch the owls,
    The wild mare in is bringing.
      Our kitchen boy hath broke his box,
      And to the dealing of the ox
      Our honest neighbors come by flocks,
    And here they will be merry.

Now kings and queens poor sheep-cotes have,
  And mate with everybody;
The honest now may play the knave,
    And wise men play at noddy.
      Some youths will now a mumming go,
      Some others play at rowland-hoe,
      And twenty other gameboys moe;
    Because they will be merry.

Then wherefore in these merry days
  Should we, I pray, be duller?
No, let us sing some roundelays
    To make our mirth the fuller.
      And whilst we thus inspired sing,
      Let all the streets with echoes ring;
      Woods, and hills, and everything
    Bear witness we are merry.

"The Minstrels played their Christmas tune"

(First three stanzas of the Dedication to *River Duddon Sonnets*)

WILLIAM WORDSWORTH (1770–1850)

The Minstrels played their Christmas tune
To-night beneath my cottage-eaves;
While, smitten by a lofty moon,
The encircling laurels, thick with leaves,
Gave back a rich and dazzling sheen,
That overpowered their natural green.

Through hill and valley every breeze
Had sunk to rest with folded wings:
Keen was the air, but could not freeze,
Nor check, the music of the strings;
So stout and hardy were the band
That scraped the chords with strenuous hand;

And who but listened?—till was paid
Respect to every Inmate's claim:
The greeting given, the music played,
In honour of each household name,
Duly pronounced with lusty call,
And "merry Christmas" wished to all!